What's Inside
Trees?

Jane Kelly Kosek

The Rosen Publishing Group's
PowerKids Press™
New York

For Beau and Abby, whose dreams include sunny days and tall trees.

Published in 1999 by The Rosen Publishing Group, Inc.
29 East 21st Street, New York, NY 10010

First Edition

Book Design: Kim Sonsky

Photo Credits: Cover, title page, contents © 1997 Digital Vision Ltd.; p. 5 © International Stock/Michele & Tom Grimm; p. 6 © FPG/Thayer Syme; p. 9 © FPG/Peter Gridley; pp. 10, 14, 17, 18 © FPG/Telegraph Colour Library; p. 13 © FPG/Ulf Sjostedt; pp. 20, 21 © 1996 PhotoDisc; p. 21 © International Stock/Scott William Hanrahan.

Kosek, Jane Kelly.
    What's inside trees? / by Jane Kelly Kosek.
        p.   cm. — (The what's inside library)
    Includes index.
    Summary: Describes what is inside trees, how they use sunlight and obtain nourishment, how they grow and reproduce, and how they can be protected in their endangered status.
    ISBN 0-8239-5281-9
    1.Trees—Juvenile literature. 2. Trees—Anatomy—Juvenile literature. [1. Trees.]
I. Title. II. Series: Kosek, Jane Kelly. What's inside library.
QK475.8.K67 1998
582.16—dc21   98-3689
                                                                        CIP
                                                                        AC

Manufactured in the United States of America

Contents

What's in a Tree?

Trees are special plants that help us in many ways. They give us food for eating, **oxygen** (AHK-sih-jen) for breathing, wood for building, paper for writing, and much more. Just by looking at a tree, you'd never know that it has a special system inside it that keeps it healthy and beautiful.

Even though a tree can be hundreds of feet tall, it has only one stem. The stem is held in the ground by roots. The upper part of the stem spreads into branches. On these branches, flowers, fruits, or leaves can grow. Some trees can grow year-round. Many, however, stop growing in the fall and shed their leaves. Then they start growing again in the spring.

Some of the tallest trees in the world are sequoias, or redwoods. They are found in California's Sequoia National Park.

Types of Trees

There are three main groups of trees: **broadleaves** (BRAWD-leevz), **conifers** (KON-ih-furz), and palms. Broadleaves have flat, wide leaves, beautiful flowers, and juicy fruits or tasty nuts. Most broadleaves are also **deciduous** (deh-SIH-joo-us) trees. Deciduous trees shed their leaves in fall.

Conifers have leaves that are scaly or look like needles. Most conifers grow cones. Trees that don't shed all their leaves at once, such as conifers, are called evergreens.

Palm trees are different from other trees. Their trunks do not grow wider with age. Instead, palm trees only grow taller. Strong **fibers** (FY-berz) protect their trunks. Also, palm trees have very large leaves and do not grow branches.

◀ Palm trees will often grow fruit, such as these coconut palm trees.

Roots

Roots are the most important part of a tree. A tree gets **minerals** (MIH-ner-ulz) and water from the soil through its roots. Roots also keep a tree from falling over.

Roots can spread out very far into the soil and they grow longer at their tips. The tips are covered with **cells** (SELZ) that protect the roots as they grow. Tiny hairs on roots collect the minerals and water from the soil.

From the root hairs, minerals and water begin a trip that will take them far up the tree to the leaves. This is where the tree's food is made.

Some trees, like this ficus tree, can develop hundreds of roots. Roots attach the tree solidly to the ground. ▶

The Trunk

The trunk is the middle section of the tree. It supports the tree and moves sap around the tree. Sap contains food, minerals, and water.

The wood at the center of the trunk is called **heartwood** (HART-wood). It supports the tree, even during strong winds, heavy rain, and blowing snow. **Sapwood** (SAP-wood) surrounds the heartwood. It contains tubes that carry the sap from the roots to the leaves and from the leaves to other parts of the tree.

As a tree grows, the trunk grows wider. A new layer of sapwood is made every year by the **cambium** (KAM-bee-um). The cambium is between the sapwood and bark. The outer layer of a tree is the bark. Bark protects all of the inner layers of the tree.

◀ You would never know just from looking at a tree that many layers exist underneath its tough bark.

Annual Rings

The many layers of wood inside the trunk are made by the cambium. If you cut across a tree's trunk, you would see layers of light and dark rings. One set of light and dark rings is a year of growth and is called an **annual ring** (AN-yoo-ul RING). The rings are smaller at the center and larger toward the bark.

A light ring is made when the tree is growing a lot. This usually happens during the spring, when there is more water for the tree. A dark ring is made during the other seasons when the tree's growth slows down. If you count the sets of light and dark rings, you will know the age of the tree.

You can count the layers inside these trees. How old are they? ▶

Branches

The upper part of a tree is made of branches that hold leaves, flowers, and fruits. Like the trunk, branches have tiny tubes through which sap, minerals, and water move.

Branches also grow new layers of wood. They grow wider and longer. Many branches stop growing during winter and form buds at their tips.

Inside the buds, new leaves and sometimes new flowers are getting ready to pop out. During spring, water from the roots carries food to the branches. This food provides the buds with energy. Then the buds break open and the branches, leaves, and flowers start to grow again!

▲ New leaves are sometimes called shoots.

Leaves

All leaves do the same thing: They make food for the tree. This food-making process is called **photosynthesis** (foh-toh-SIN-thuh-sis).

There are many steps in photosynthesis. Each leaf contains a green coloring called **chlorophyll** (KLOR-uh-fil). When the sun shines on a leaf, the leaf's chlorophyll takes energy from sunlight. With this energy, the leaf makes food for the tree. It mixes the gas **carbon dioxide** (KAR-bin dy-OK-syd) from the air with water from the soil. The leaf also gives off oxygen. After the food is made, **veins** (VAYNZ) inside the leaf move it to the rest of the tree. The veins also move water from the roots to all parts of the leaves.

Leaves help people and animals by releasing oxygen into the air. We need oxygen to breathe. ▶

Cones, Flowers, and Fruits

Every tree first begins as a seed. But where does the seed come from?

A seed is made inside a cone or flower that grows on the branch of a tree. A cone usually has either a male or female part. Most flowers have both male and female parts. When a female part gets **pollen** (PAH-lun) from a male part, one or more seeds can start to grow.

As seeds grow inside a flower, the flower changes and becomes a fleshy fruit or a hard nut. The fruit or nut will protect the seeds. A cone gets harder to protect growing seeds. As it gets harder, it changes from green to brown.

When seeds leave the tree, they may fall to the ground and grow into new trees.

◀ Even a seedling of this size could grow into a tree that's one hundred feet tall.

Trees as Homes

Many living things, such as birds, squirrels, and insects, make their homes inside trees. The birds may build nests and lay eggs on the branches or inside the trunk. Squirrels may live and hide their food for the winter inside a hole in a tree. Insects may eat a tree's wood. This is important for keeping a balance in nature. But a tree must also protect itself so it does not get sick.

The bark of a tree is made to protect the inside of a tree. When something breaks through the bark, the inside of the tree can become sick and die. Some trees are able to fight illness better than others. Some can even cover holes in their bark with **resin** (REZ-in).

Some frogs will climb out to the edge of a tree branch to snack on insects that are living there.

20

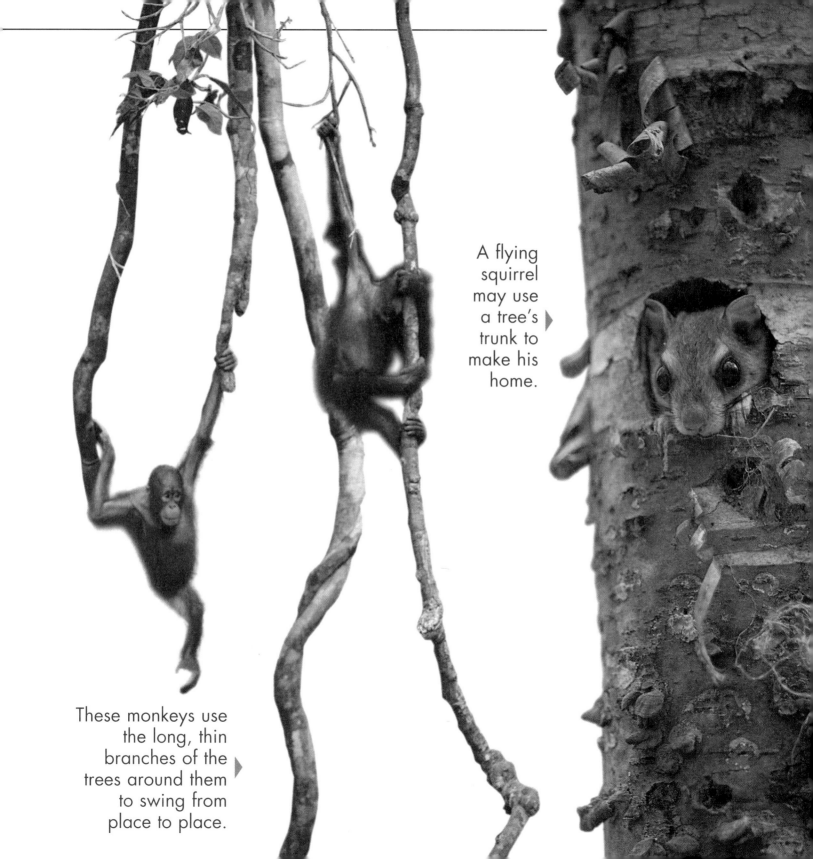

A flying squirrel may use a tree's trunk to make his home. ▶

These monkeys use the long, thin branches of the trees around them ▶ to swing from place to place.

Protecting Trees

Trees are made up of many different parts that work together to make a tree strong and healthy.

Because trees give us so much, we need to protect them. A great way to help trees is by planting more trees and by **recycling** (ree-SY-kling) paper in your home and school. You can also remember these tips:

- Do not tear off any bark, branches, or leaves from a tree
- Do not attach anything to a tree
- Do not build a fire too close to a tree

If we learn to take care of trees, they will continue to take care of us.

Web Sites:

You can find out more about trees at these Web sites:
http://www.sufa.com/
http://www.trees.org/

Glossary

annual ring (AN-yoo-ul RING) A set of light and dark rings in a tree's trunk that are made by the tree during each year of its life.

broadleaf (BRAWD-leef) A type of tree that has flat, wide leaves, grows flowers and fruits or nuts, and usually sheds its leaves in the fall.

cambium (KAM-bee-um) The layer of cells between the bark and the sapwood that produces new growth.

carbon dioxide (KAR-bin dy-OK-syd) A colorless gas that leaves take in from the air to help them make food for the tree.

cell (SEL) A basic building block of all living things.

chlorophyll (KLOR-uh-fil) A green coloring in leaves that allows them to use energy from sunlight to make food.

conifer (KON-ih-fur) A type of tree that has needlelike leaves and grows cones.

deciduous (deh-SIH-joo-us) A type of tree that sheds its leaves in fall.

fiber (FY-ber) A small part of a palm tree that looks like a thread.

heartwood (HART-wood) The wood core that supports a tree.

mineral (MIH-ner-ul) Something that occurs in nature and is not a plant, animal, or other living thing.

oxygen (AHK-sih-jen) A colorless gas that is released by leaves into the air, which many living things need to breathe.

photosynthesis (foh-toh-SIN-thuh-sis) The process in which leaves use energy from sunlight, gases from air, and water from soil to make food and release oxygen.

pollen (PAH-lun) A powder that is released by the male part of a flower. If it reaches the female part of a flower, it can cause seeds to begin growing in that flower.

recycling (ree-SY-kling) To reuse.

resin (REZ-in) A sticky liquid that some trees release to cover holes in their bark.

sapwood (SAP-wood) The wood in a tree that carries sap.

vein (VAYN) A narrow channel in a leaf.

Index

7/00

DATE DUE

AUG 2 5 2000	
9/02/00	
SEP 0 8 2000	
APR 1 8 2002	